THE
CARIBBEAN

Gospel and Culture pamphlets:

GOSPEL AND CULTURES PAMPHLET 10

THE CARIBBEAN

Enculturation, Acculturation and the Role of the Churches

Lewin L. Williams

WCC Publications, Geneva

Cover design: Edwin Hassink
Cover photo: WCC

ISBN 2-8254-1201-5

© 1996 WCC Publications, World Council of Churches,
150 route de Ferney, 1211 Geneva 2, Switzerland

No. 10 in the Gospel and Cultures series

Printed in Switzerland

Table of Contents

Introduction

The Reformation position that faith is a divine gift served originally as an extra ballast in the doctrine of justification, to ensure that there is no salvation by works. By the time the missionaries introduced it to the Caribbean, it was meant to limit salvation purely to the soul; hence the gospel was never related to the physical condition of its hosts. Sealed and signed as that idea may have been, however, it could not deter the questions it raised. The assurance that not even faith must have human origins, lest it too be considered an achievement such as work, failed to explain the absence of the reward for the kind of labour which slavery and indentureship forced upon their victims. Even more troublesome is the series of faith questions which arose regarding its nature as a divine gift:

— What is the warrant for the gift? In view of the many religious forms in the Caribbean and the extra-European influences in Christianity itself, to whom is faith given and why?
— Does faith refer to concrete realities in the community?
— Do people other than Christians receive it?
— How is it serviced through the community that is not Christian, or the community that holds religious categories beyond the boundaries of Christianity?

Whatever may be the answers to these questions, it is safe to say that faith is not only based on concrete reality but is also moulded and shaped by the concreteness of context. Faith cannot eject from its context; and within the pluralism of the Caribbean situation, faith questions are never smooth and the answers are never easy. Therefore, much is at stake for the Christian gospel in addressing the questions concerning faith and religious pluralism.

Today, when interfaith dialogue is possible, civility and respect are observed especially among the major religions such as Christianity, Islam, Bahai, Hinduism and Buddhism. Furthermore, mutuality in liberation struggles means that the Rastafarian movement, which has led the way in race and class protest, has been included in the interfaith relations where matters of faith are discussed. But this interaction promises peaceful coexistence only as long as no attempt is made to broach the subject of ascendancy in the validity of faith among "faiths". The problem of absolutization stands ready to create "existential disruptions". Every religious entity is aware of its presence, making itself a real source of tension among the faiths.

In the Caribbean, however, the greater tension lies in the existence of certain other religious forms which touch — or are touched by — Christianity "in the dark", so to speak. These forms have not earned the respect accorded by missionary Christianity to the "major" religions, and they have been stigmatized as the "shadowy activities of pagan societies". Yet they are important to many individuals, even at the risk of being ostracized by the Christian community, which is always in mortal dread of "syncretism". Undeniably, these religious forms are gaining some recognition because they are associated with cultural survival, and because they service (albeit underground) the need for some practical demonstration of the availability of religious benefits not addressed in missionary Christianity. In addition, the dominance of Christianity dictates that those who insist on accessing their favours develop a kind of *sotto voce* approach to any sympathy towards these forms. Thus tensions develop between the persistence of these forms and the dominance of the Christian attitude towards them. We label them "tensions of faith" with the presumption that faith, even as a given, does not belong exclusively to Christianity, and also that what is caught between Christianity and other religious forms is faith in ambivalence in relation to authority.

Would this weighty ambivalence have arisen if Christianity had not made its advent in the Caribbean through the bias of European acculturation? Indeed, would these forms have survived if the social application of the gospel had covered the indigenous need for the practicalities of faith found in the other religious forms? Is the gospel responsible for any of the cultural revolution that flouts the authority of state and church alike in the Caribbean reality today?

This essay examines the precipitation into contemporary times of faith tensions from the historical patterns of enculturation and acculturation. It will assess the effect of the faith tensions which have developed in:

— the process of Caribbean indigenization through theological perspectives;

— the secret participation of Christians in pre-colonial religious forms which have survived colonial domination;

— the raucous demonstration of cultural disengagement, which defies the role of the church in the maintenance of values and value systems, arising out of serious ambivalence among persons caught in a hybrid culture created out of enculturation and acculturation.

In conclusion a biblical paradigm will be lifted up as a way of connecting the imperatives the gospel may have, especially for the Caribbean.

1. Caribbean Enculturation

Enculturation is the natural process of socialization that belongs to a particular culture: the acquiring and passing on of the traditional specifics which belong to the culture, so that the culture is continued from generation to generation. If there is a Caribbean culture, it is enculturation which determines it. Enculturation, which can be both a conscious and an unconscious process, covers all of life. For example, it covers the area of music, claiming it, branding it and perpetuating it. Calypso sound, rhythm and steel band speak of Trinidad and Tobago. Reggae music, for all of its universal penetration, belongs to Jamaica. Similarly, distinctions in culinary art create cultural particularity. Choice of mate and sexual patterns have cultural inducement through succeeding generations.

Difficulties arise because an enormous amount of *acculturation* — that is, imposition of other cultures from outside — has gone into the formation of the codes by which the Caribbean people have lived over time. In addition to this acculturation, "Caribbean culture" itself has a multiplicity of roots.

Some have argued that determining what is authentic in Caribbean or any other culture is the work of sociologists and anthropologists. However, since many other analysts must constantly make references to the concreteness of the Caribbean culture, it is not only sociologists and anthropologists who confront the issue of the significance of its diverse roots, genesis and ultimate recognizable characteristics. One discipline which has wrestled with the problem of identifying what is truly Caribbean in terms of its culture is Caribbean theology.

Caribbean theology is involved in this process because of its interest in disengaging from those colonial patterns of religion which depreciate efforts at self-actualization among the people. In addition, Caribbean theology is itself a new process of enculturation, since its special focus is indigenization.

The idea of disengagement demands a programme of self-understanding. Indeed, a process of religious introspection in search of cultural identity began in the early 1970s, after the Black Power movement charged quite convincingly that the gospel which came to the Caribbean by way of Europe arrived in European cultural garb and that from its arrival in the Caribbean it was an instrument for social control used against the colonized people in general and the slaves in particular. Hence even theologians are involved in identifying what is Caribbean culture and how it is affected by religion. But the variety of ethnic roots in the Caribbean reality has made this a difficult task.

Out of Many One People

The phrase "Out of Many One People" is a borrowed one. It belongs to the Jamaican people as their national motto. It resembles that of the United States, *E Pluribus Unum*: out of many one. The difference between the Jamaican and US versions is that in the latter, "many" refers to the individual states and "one" to the federal composite, whereas in Jamaica the emphasis is on people, and the "many" refers to its citizenry, which is made up of several ethnic groups. Considering how the process of evolution in the Caribbean has gone, one can easily apply this concept to the whole region. Although territorial political constraints cause constant shifts in emphasis back and forth from the "one" to the "many", what is true of the Jamaican composite is true of the Caribbean as a whole.

The culture of the region began with the Arawaks and Caribs who occupied the land before the Spanish invasion. And while it is true that this invasion caused the annihilation of the original inhabitants in most of the territories, it was not before they had made some permanent cultural contribution to their successors. Some of this legacy comprises food, language, vocabulary and patterns of living. Each of the succeeding groups — Africans, Indians, Chinese and Europeans — has added to that legacy in distinctive ways of life. To a certain extent, these have merged into the development of a shared reality. Thus in the case of food, a meal of rice, cassava bread (bammy) and curried goat's meat is an amalgamated cultural product of the Arawaks, Africans, Indians and Chinese.

Unfortunately, to move beyond the harmony of culinary art, and to add the European segment, is to move from enculturation to acculturation. This assessment is based on the fact that the European segment introduced colonialism, slavery and racism, making it responsible for the cultural stratification and domination which have made disengagement a viable alternative to what could otherwise have been a harmonious amalgamation. This is the basic problem with Caribbean identity.

It is no wonder that the presentation of the gospel has reaped animosity, because it arrived with the dominating culture and with much of the same philosophy and many of the same attitudes. In fact, the Caribbean was never without religion. Enculturation — that is, socialization in all the various aspects of the particular culture — incorporated the pre-colonial rootedness of religious consciousness. Indeed, when Columbus arrived in the Caribbean he became convinced that his hosts were aware of transcendence, because they mistook him and his crew for messengers of the heavenly God. Columbus' immediate conclusion was that Christianity would be readily cultivated among the Arawaks because they demonstrated religious propensity marked by civil behaviour. He was certain that there was going to be easy compliance when he noticed that there was a remarkable absence of idols. Of course it is now a documented fact that the Arawaks believed in a transcendent being called Jocahuma who, though omnipotent, was attributed with the same kind of gentleness and kindness after which their own lives were patterned. On the other hand, the Caribs, who were not quite as gentle, believed that there was an unidentifiable force behind the earth which saw to the provision of all that was necessary for life (Dale Bisnauth, *History of Religions in the Caribbean*).

Even if there were no evidence of pre-colonial religiosity among the Africans, who were the next group to arrive, it would have to be assumed that they brought religious forms to the "New World". In many of the African territories from which they hailed, there were organized religions, complete with observances, rituals and worship. Only people who were accustomed to religious observances could have connected as quickly as some African slaves did to the Christian rituals which the missionaries introduced. For example, baptism by immersion in rivers had such a quick and ready appeal to them that it was bound to have been connected to something in their own religious experience. Indeed, there is now ample evidence that with the Africans a number of religious forms came to the Caribbean which have survived to one degree of intensity or another.

Generally speaking, then, the original people of the Caribbean, as well as the earliest addition, the Africans, were people of religion. They had been going through the same evolutionary processes which religiosity takes in any given human society. And subsequent scholarship has shown that with some Africans a fully organized religion such as Islam arrived in the Caribbean. Later on, with the advent of labour contracts in indentured services, the Indians and Chinese introduced Hinduism, Buddhism and more of Islam.

There are different ways today of assessing religious cooperation, but it can safely be said that when the gospel was introduced in the religious complexity of the Caribbean, its severest idiosyncrasy was the fear of syncretism. That fear pushed it to condemn and avoid what it did not know. Needless to say, the attitude of condemnation not only expressed itself in claims of superiority, but also resulted in the assertion by European mission of an imperial right to religious consciousness and observances in the region. The gospel itself thus became a tool for acculturation.

2. Acculturation in the Caribbean

Acculturation, as we have said, is the imposition of distinctly forcing one culture upon another. To be sure, there are cases in which acculturation is not forced: one can speak of voluntary acculturation in which one culture allows a "benign imposition" of patterns from another culture upon itself. In the case of colonization and enslavement, however, acculturation is meant to erase the host culture to the benefit of the dominant.

In the Caribbean, acculturation began in earnest the moment Columbus made the decision to exploit his hosts. His records include the observations that the Arawaks neither bore arms, nor seemed to know them, and that they were very intelligent people who would make excellent servants. The contention that the introduction of the gospel was wedded to economic expansion is thus warranted from the very beginning. Since the Arawaks learned as quickly as they did and apparently had no idols, Columbus believed they would make good Christians. He observed further that they could be taught Spanish and how to be obedient, and that some of them wore articles of gold and should be induced to reveal the source of it. Here then are the ingredients which worked together to create the dominating process of acculturation: economics, cultural stratification and God.

Colonialism and slavery are elements of a superior/inferior equation. For colonization and enslavement to take place, the cultural inferiority of the colonized must be assumed by the colonizers. This is implicit in Columbus' immediate assessment that the Arawaks would make good servants. Despite the possibility mentioned above of self-imposed and benign acculturation, therefore, in the case of the Caribbean it was clearly an imposition detrimental to the cultural stability of the victims. This is the case, whether one is referring to the actual physical colonial invasion or to the debilitating strategy of neo-colonialism to "adjust" economies to the benefit of the dominant culture. In either case, acculturation is an exercise of power that is detrimental to the host culture and often leaves protracted psychological effects in the form of a lack of self-actualizing creativity.

If we look at two other layers of immigrant culture in the Caribbean — African and Indian — we see further detrimental effects of acculturation. The problem of domination was compounded when the introduction of black slavery brought the Africans to the Caribbean shores. Being uprooted and transported into situations extrinsic to their original culture placed them at an even greater disadvantage than the indigenous inhabitants, subjecting them to the kind of disorientation which creates and maintains powerlessness.

While it is true that the Indians came to the Caribbean with labour contracts in hand, it gradually dawned on them that they too were suffering from cultural dislocation. They received much less than their contracts promised, and depressing social conditions severely affected their family structures. Plantation owners who were accustomed to mistreating slaves could not resist the temptation of treating their Indian employees as slaves. They often whipped them. In fact the situation deteriorated to such an extent that the Indian government was forced to intervene on behalf of its nationals. Indeed, some Caribbean historians now refer to this period as "the other slavery".

Pertinent to our discussion at this juncture is the question of how the gospel affected this situation for change.

3. Tensions in Faith and Culture

The gospel, by its very nature, is meant to be transported. The justification for its existence, focus and function is its communicability. Even the most contextual discussions in missiology will concede that the *missio Dei* ("mission of God") is most significant in its global reference. Therefore the problem with the missionary enterprise in the Caribbean has never been with the mere arrival of the gospel. The problem has been twofold. First of all, the extent to which the gospel was confused with missionary culture is of grave concern. Given the missionaries' claim that their culture was at the apex of cultural stratification, and the reality of the resulting cultural domination, the question is whether the host cultures have not been misevangelized. Second, the application of the gospel to "concerns of the soul" — to the almost total neglect of social needs — caused a faulty praxis to develop. That praxis ignored the self-actualization of the people whom the missionaries saw as a mission field to be "saved".

The possibility of misevangelization

Cultural imposition as the focus of proselytization is as old as the gospel itself. Jesus, being conscious of how negatively the practice affected people, chided the Pharisaic community for the imposition: "For you cross sea and land to make a single convert, and you make the new convert twice as much a child of hell as yourselves" (Matt. 23:15). Here we note that there is no serious objection to the missionary venture as such. Rather, it is the cultural imposition which this venture practises — in the belief that its culture is normative — that makes the negative difference: "you make the new convert twice as much a child of hell as yourselves."

Indeed, while drastic changes have taken place in the areas of liturgy and mission strategy in the so-called "mother" churches in Europe and North America, the missionary churches in the Caribbean have remained almost as colonial as the day they were started. It is not unusual for denominations considered to be "enlightened" to hold "missionary services" during which one can hear vivid renditions of songs, written a century and more ago to encourage those who would bring the light of the gospel to their ancestors, which are replete with the missionary presumption of godlessness and ignorance. Even today people seem to derive spiritual blessing from lyrics such as these:

> *In heathen lands afar*
> *Thick darkness broodeth yet;*
> *Arise, O Morning Star,*
> *Arise and never set.*

They sing, apparently oblivious to the fact that there are now skyscrapers in many of the cities of the continent to which these lines refer, the continent of their own cultural heritage. Only in worship would these "enlightened Christians" overlook the fact that calling Africa the "dark continent" is cultural diminution. In other words, people who have been socialized by the gospel have to accept not only being belittled by others, but also to belittle themselves. Such people are misevangelized.

Therefore, the problem of misevangelization should not be considered as something that took place in the past and therefore is now among the innocuous relics of ancient history. The problem is as alive today as when the conquistadors arrived with the Bible in one hand and the sword in the other to conduct a "violent evangelism". For there are "new missionaries" in action in the Caribbean as in many developing countries of the world. They are usually armed with the kind of fundamentalism which is camouflaged as an "apolitical" gospel. Yet, given the conservative nature of this neopietism and the swiftness and pervasiveness of its development, especially in the wake of the stumbling of the Marxist left, the activity of these new missionaries deserves close scrutiny. They arrive from cultures in which the market economy prevails with an agenda that gives priority to postponing the liberation of the poor to otherworldly times and heavenly destinations. Maintaining a cold war mentality with regards to cultural and political polarization, they impose their own political and economic philosophy upon their hosts, promoting it, if not as synonymous with the gospel, then as a prominent part of it. They consider it a divinely appointed duty to pray and preach innovative governments out of office, so that their cultural and political machinations may be accepted without examination and opposition.

Even on the question of evangelization, then, there is good reason to insist that economics be included in any examination of the impact of the gospel on contemporary society, especially societies of the developing world. As M. Douglas Meeks discusses thoroughly in *God the Economist*, it has been abundantly demonstrated in the Bible that "economy" is part of the divine concern. Since there is such a reality as *oikonomia tou Theou* ("the economy of God"), the gospel of Jesus Christ must attend to it. And if people are evangelized into separating gospel from their social, economic and political realities, that evangelization process is faulty.

The gospel in praxis

No Caribbean person would wish for a gospel that comes with no imperative for *metanoia* (repentance and change). There is no culture so perfect that its values may not be criticized for moral failures within. Ideas of right and wrong are present in all cultures, creating possibilities for the conviction of *sin*, guilt and positive adjustments in ways of thinking and living. One of the criticisms leveled against liberation theology is that it does not address the problem of sin within the oppressed community. The counter-claim made in Caribbean liberation theology is that sin has been amply addressed in its significance as *hamartia*, which in most instances means the failure to struggle for an affirmation of the image of God within the oppressed self. The reasoning behind this approach to interpreting the concept of sin is to avoid the psychological effects of further condemnation of the very people who have always been the victims of condemnation in society. The *hamartia* principle, therefore, while acknowledging human failure, points immediately to the positive challenge in the struggle to reach one's highest potential. Even so, the gospel has to be heard for its spiritual and practical emphases in that challenge towards being and doing better.

Yet the Christianity that begins by ignoring the context of its hosts, while imposing new cultural life-styles at will and by whim, is behaving in an imperialistic way. The very sense of conviction regarding sin is so fraught with cultural biases that the whole concept of rightness and wrongness in given cultures calls for contextual interpretations. The variations in the Caribbean mix itself create that necessity. In the case of language and meaning the differences are clear. In Jamaica "bullah" is an innocent reference to a small round cake, a part of the unique culinary contribution to Caribbean culture. In Barbados "bullah" (same word) is a crude reference to homosexuality.

Needless to say, in interpreting the gospel from a missionary perspective a word could have an entirely different meaning from that which it bears for the host culture. Nobody seems to know why, but the word "forgery" in rural Jamaica used to mean rape. Someone using the word in its economic sense would convey a totally different meaning to the rural hearer. How much greater the potential for misunderstanding in the kind of gospel interpretation represented by the cultural confrontation between a missionary from a culture whose aversion to any open demonstration of sensuality extended to covering even the legs of a piano, and a woman from the host culture in which it was considered normal to leave the breasts uncovered. Or think of what damage is done to the psyche of people of colour when the missionary church insists that white is the only symbol of purity acceptable to God, so for holy communion and other special services the dress must be white and the important lyrics for the occasion include "Wash me and I shall be whiter than snow". This indicates that gospel in praxis may be more inappropriate than it is casually observed to be.

To this day there are some missionary churches in which persons who retain some memory of their pre-colonial roots experience a sense of spiritual and social discomfort. One reason for this is that the same process for cultural and social stratification employed in colonial politics has been employed by segments of the missionary church in the promotion of the gospel. This is certainly the case where the church makes no attempt at understanding the pre-colonial religious patterns in its constituency, when it dismisses as mere superstition that which it does not understand, when it imposes a brand of Christianity which is still steeped in imported cultural trappings on the unresolved tensions of the religious situation.

As Abraham Maslow has demonstrated in *Motivation and Personality*, different cultures have different ways of satisfying the same need. Anthropologically speaking, there are scarcely any differences among the fundamental desires of all human beings; but out of different psychologies, owing to the cultural differences in socialization, two different cultures may employ completely different ways of fulfilling those desires. Self-esteem is one area in which this has been observed. In all cultures there is the need for self-esteem, but what it takes to fulfil that need can differ drastically from culture to culture. It all depends on the values and systems of meaning with which a particular culture operates. Here there should be no judgmental questions regarding better or worse, as far as these values and systems of meaning are concerned. The important issue of which those who apply the gospel must be aware is that there are differences among cultures. In the Caribbean situation the gospel applied without this con-textual sensitivity has developed some adverse reactions.

Backlash to faulty evangelism praxis

Developments over time have highlighted the existence and deep significance of some residual attitudes that have been assessed as a backlash to colonial evangelization: (1) the indigenization of social and theological perspectives; (2) the recondite but practical use made by some, including members of sophisticated US groups in church and society, of persistent religious US forms from pre-colonial cultures; (3) the explosive clash of values in the cultural hybridity between Caribbean enculturation and European acculturation.

The indigenization of theology

An attendant feature of the emphasis on self-understanding is the re-evaluation of enculturated patterns and forms. For example, the folk traditions become of paramount importance. Folk dialect, folklore, culinary art, music and representational art all go through a real renaissance. Folk culture which was once shelved in deference to the "cultured" acceptance of art forms of the dominant culture, is revived into meaningfulness. Religious forms such as *obeah*, revivalism, *cuminah*, *shango* and voodoo have gained some positive recognition.

Revivalism as a religious form has had its most significant development in post-emancipation Jamaica. The "revival" fulfilled the desire to recover the spirituality which was lost as part of the cultural destruction that took place during slavery. It began with a tremendous surge of energy employed to transform protracted pain. It included rituals for both worship and healing, seeking practical benefits to the whole person. Though revivalism is a post-emancipation phenomenon, it draws upon the African cultural bearing for its sustenance and meaning.

The word *cuminah* probably means "to dance", and its practice as a religious form has its roots in Africa. The rituals are often mistakenly judged as mere ancestor worship. However, when Queenie, a *cuminah* practitioner and interpreter, was interviewed she stated that the spirits of the ancestors are participants in the human community. They have more wisdom and power to deal with the world, so the rituals are meant to encourage them to make intercession on behalf of the bodied living. Some ecumenical rituals demonstrate the harmony that must be preserved between humanity and nature. For instance, if a tree must be felled for the making of ceremonial drums, there is a ceremony acknowledging the pain caused to both the tree and nature. Part of this ritual involves burying something valuable in the soil as an act of atonement for a regrettable deed.

Shango is the name of the God of Thunder, belief in whom originated in West Africa with the Yoruba. The power of *shango* is demonstrated through lightning which is interpreted as a fiery axe hurled from heaven by the god. In *Shango* ritual the worshippers dance and sing to the music of the drum, which creates a suspension from temporal reality in which spiritual focus may set in. In this state they may receive special revelations which make clear for them how the physical world may be dealt with.

This Yoruba god Shango has been adopted in a kind of Caribbean "syncretism" that has been popularized primarily in Trinidad and Grenada. "Syncretism" here is not used pejoratively, but refers to drawing on other religions in the establishment of a core of faith. In this religious form the spirit world has strong ties with the world of "fleshly" existence and the spirits (which are not gods, though they related to the divine Shango) are called upon to perform healing within the community. There is also a negative side, in which the spirits are called upon to bring retaliatory evil on enemies as a form of "justifiable" retribution.

Though Shango is the God of Thunder, the primary divine attribute is not violence but power. Therefore, as powerful as the leadership in this religious form is, its membership is motivated toward pride and self-worth. In fact, that pride and self-worth are not grounded in some abstract spirituality, but in the fact of their connection with the Yoruba people. *Shango* rose to its highest peak of popularity in Trinidad in the late 1960s, just prior to the time the Black Power movement flared, with its doctrine of disengagement from colonially influenced religious forms and colonial patterns of living. It has been suggested, therefore, that the Black Power movement was strongly influenced by the *shango* religion.

At one level, the renaissance of these religious forms has been part of a cultural renaissance, particularly by providing subject matter for the performing arts. At another leve, this has been important for the decolonizing and indigenizing process. From a theological and sociological perspective, the survival of these religious forms has been viewed as providing sound evidence of the indomitable nature of the human spirit, even under the forces of negative evangelization and the harshest forms of colonial resocialization. It was their fear of conspiracy among the African people that lay behind the colonizers' decision to eradicate their culture. If the people were not permitted to speak their own language it meant that they had to speak a language the colonizer understood and could thus monitor. When they lost the memory of their culture, the process of colonization was complete. They became more adaptable in the new orientation, and therefore more manageable. The church found colonizing convenient because it did not wish to deal with the paganism it perceived these cultures to contain. Historically speaking, though, there were cases in which total acculturation was more a wish in the mind of the colonizers than a reality in the heart of the African.

It is now well-known that the Africans developed such creative ways of using the master's language that the master heard the words but missed the meaning in the construction. Needless to say, some religious principles and observances were just too tenacious to disappear. And this is exactly one of the signs observed by the thrust for indigenization: that self-determination can be a post-colonial reality. This is why Caribbean theology has warned consistently that it is important for the missionary church to understand these religious forms. It insists that indigenization should mean much more than avoiding liturgical material meant for foreign contexts.

Caribbean theology has called for the erasure of language that evokes negative memories of domination and servitude. More than anything else, indigenization means decolonization to the core of the spiritual, social, economic and political significance of the gospel, and also the Caribbeanization of the church's witness to the same gospel. It means further that the re-mythologization of some pre-colonial traditions should be activated for the benefit they can produce for the self-actualization of the Caribbean community. So stories are part of the methodology of indigenization in the Caribbean. For people who had distinct claims to oral traditions, recalling the stories which lie latent in the cultural psyche is the intentional revival of culture.

Recondite use of religious forms

To portray these extra-colonial religious forms in the performing arts and or to use them as topics for academic discussion is one thing. It is quite another to accept them openly as bona fide religion in a sharply classist post-colonial society. Yet even some highly sophisticated persons will seek the services of unconventional religious centres. One reason for this is the need for more practical demonstrations of the faith and faith response in the life of the ordinary Christian believer.

Take the matter of health and healing, for example. The missionary church has never seriously focused on physical healing in ministry. Anthony Allen, physician, psychiatrist and theologian, argues in *Health, Healing and Transformation* that the gospel call to healing ministries has been left by the missionary church to either charlatans or professionals. And the church has done this out of an uninformed acceptance of the Cartesian split between mind and body, therefore between spirit and matter. When matter was the evil thing in the prevailing worldview the church promoted it, so as not to lose the significance of the incarnation of Jesus Christ as spirit in flesh. Once matter came to be more important than ideas of the spirit through the predominance of the scientific worldview, the church began to emphasize the spiritual to the exclusion of the material, and in so doing has failed in its healing responsibility to the body.

But the need of course does not die just because the church avoids it. Members of the church turn elsewhere because some of the extra-colonial religious forms, for example *obeah*, invoke supernatural powers in the healing of the body. Certainly there are charlatans in this field. Certainly there is the confusion of divine spirit with the spirits of the dead. Certainly the repertoire of the practitioners contains supernatural curses as well as supernatural blessings, revenge in the name of justice as well as care. However, because they offer some practical considerations beyond those offered by the gospel as it has been presented, in merely theoretical and "spiritual" terms, people seek their assistance. The appeal is recondite but the church is aware that it exists, and the church's highbrow response creates enough guilt in the seekers of this healing to cause conflicts of faith. The question is whether the gospel itself stands in judgment against the participants. In fact, when the followers of Jesus objected to a healing ministry that was being performed by others who did not belong to the fold, Jesus himself saw no need for concern. Indeed he interpreted it as support for his cause.

A cursory study of culture and religions shows that none of the contexts from which the colonized immigrants were brought to the Caribbean promoted separation between religion on the one hand and day-to-day living on the other. In fact in these contexts religion provided the philosophy of life. People simply lived by their religious convictions. This was true of Africa as it was of India and China. Therefore an African religious form such as *obeah*, as practised in the Caribbean, is the consciousness of a certain connectionalism that exists among all facets of life.

The practice is spoken of as *science*, and it is necessary to point out here that *science* is different from *seance*. Science may have something to do with a seance, but science is a much wider concept than the spiritualism of seance. In its practice science is believed to be the acquisition of exceptional skills, and these skills accumulate out of both spiritual gifts of discernment and the acquiring of special kinds of knowledge. This knowledge includes an understanding of how the universe came into being; the genesis and relations of good and evil in the world; how humanity was created; how things are connected spiritually and physically; how to explain historical occurrences through the principles of cause and effect; how spirit is able to cause transformation in matter, and therefore how to effect and explain equations between illness and wellness, brokenness and wholeness.

While the activities of these differing religious forms are not monolithic in meaning or method, scholarship has highlighted some facts about them. It had long been thought that the African immigrants to the Caribbean came exclusively from the northwest coast of Africa. However by residual language patterns and vocabulary it is now known that they came from all over the continent. Some vocabulary and practices seem to relate some of the surviving religious forms in the Caribbean to as far away as the Bantu lands in Africa.

In some rural villages in Jamaica the word *kuntu* is used in ordinary speech, usually to seal a covenant, especially among children at play. According to Ivor Morrish in *Obeah, Christ and Rastaman*, *kuntu* is a prominent concept in Bantu philosophy. The system begins with *ntu*, a force which infuses all existence — in the same sense as the original movers of the *logos* theory thought of it. And *ntu* is the basic root word from which *bantu, muntu, kintu, hantu* and *kuntu* are derived. Once the meaning of each word is understood, it can be seen how they work in the Bantu philosophy of life, and also how the philosophy is distilled through the science that has been under discussion.

Kintu refers to the intelligence that flows through all things. *Hantu* is used in reference to the dimensions of time and space. And as it informs "the very modality of life", it is *kuntu*. *Bantu* is human being, and *muntu* is humanity in the plural sense. The root word *ntu* ensures the idea that every single area of life is under a comprehensive connectional system. As a result of this connectional system, there is nothing without a cause. Illness is caused by something within the system, and therefore certain areas of the same system must be manipulated for healing.

One should not get the impression that all the residual religious forms are like *obeah*, nor that *obeah* has only to do with illness and wellness. But what it has in common with some of the other religious forms is an interest in the interaction between the supernatural and the natural. For example, what the New Testament has to say about "principalities and powers" beyond the conclave of "flesh and blood" bears interest for *obeah*, for this concept evokes metaphysical contemplation that brings the Bible into focus, using it to bring some divine authority to many of the activities in this science.

Though the church personalizes evil in the form of Satan, it basically holds to a Westernized mindset regarding the spirit world whenever the idea of spirit is generated from non-European contexts. Hence faith conflicts always arise around interpretations of the three-dimensional understanding of community as the living, the dead and the yet-to-be. Even more of a contradiction is the fact that the church in its doctrine of *communion of saints* claims a union between living saints and saints who are beyond the grave.

Caribbean Christianity is now no less afraid of syncretism than when Columbus first landed in 1492. Yet there are those who insist that the church owes it to its context to investigate the needs that exist by virtue of a cultural development in the psyche of many people.

4. Decolonization and Cultural Hybridity

Caribbean people have a way of putting their peculiar stamp on acculturation of any kind. For example, in every English-speaking Caribbean territory perfect English among the folk can be spoken with a "Caribbean accent". Standardized European fare is taken over in Caribbean culinary art and its flavour is made distinctively Caribbean. Dance patterns developed in Europe have been stamped with Caribbean rhythm. Folk traditions out of colonialism have been Caribbeanized and made part of local tradition. Despite the cultural superiority claimed by the European immigrants to the Caribbean, the reality among the people of the Caribbean suggests that there was not always sexual containment within the European cultures. This indicates that acculturation may sometimes harmonize very well with enculturation, to the extent that some analysts speak of "Afro-Saxon" and "Indo-Saxon" in reference to some Caribbean persons. This is cultural hybridity, when people are influenced by more than one culture. Unfortunately, we must admit that it does not always produce harmony.

When in the decolonization and indigenization process the immigrants, especially the Africans, recall the forced loss of cultural traditions, serious anger can develop. In recent times the pendulum swing in this area has caused the emergence of behaviour that has been classified as extremely crude and vulgar.

Perhaps there is no gentle way to demonstrate the will to be independent after being under colonial power for some of the longest years in modern history. The political break from Europe came by negotiation, but the psychological break has been quite another matter, requiring much more self-persuasion. For example, when the University of the West Indies got caught up in the winds of self-determination, the students did not just stop wearing academic robes to classes. They employed more drastic means to bring a colonial practice to an end. To break the psychological dependency they had to burn the robes.

As people become more self-assured, the disengagement becomes more noticeable as the objective permeates all of society. Interestingly enough, it was in the early 1970s, concurrently with the rise of black power in the region, that the Caribbean church began for the first time to re-examine the theology it had inherited from the missionary thrust. And in that black power movement there were drastic demonstrations of the dislike for things colonial. As some of the church's own colonial relics became defaced, the church sat up and took notice. Of course, the Caribbean theology which developed out of this re-examination has always been far more radical in its support of disengagement than the rank-and-file church leadership has been willing to participate in. Yet today, even that radical perspective is showing concern over a society that exhibits very little desire for elegance and gentility, because it associates elegance and gentility with the colonial acculturation of docility in those whom they the colonized.

Values in a colonial system may have been based on the colonizers' sense of value which, as we have seen, seldom operates in support of the colonized. As necessary as it is to radicalize disengagement from the colonial experience, however, it must be done without the kind of pervasive vulgarity that leads to self-destruction in regard to the values of enculturation. But self-destruction does not seem to worry some segments of contemporary Caribbean society, as long as behaviour patterns repulse what the colonizer expected of the colonized.

While the church formerly exercised a validating role for moral values, in many areas of the society it is now in danger of being sidelined. Many charges are being levelled anew at the missionary church, which is said to have made too many bad judgments: (1) It aided and abetted the colonizing forces against the welfare of the host people. (2) It bears direct responsibility for the advent and prolongation of slavery in the region. (3) It emphasized the spiritual dimension of the gospel out of all proportion to its social, economic and political message, presenting a message that was quick to address the freedom of souls but slow to raise the issue of freedom from the bondage of real chains. (4) When neo-colonialism replaced colonial occupation, the missionary church failed to engage itself in advocating the eradication of poverty; instead, it used its energy to enter the major power debate on totalitarian leadership in obstruction of the divinely ordered free market system. (5) It allowed the capitalist culture to be shaded into the broader definitions of Christianity, so that certain kinds of political innovations in the region may be destabilized in the name of Christ.

These charges are not new; some of them obviously go back as far as the Spanish incursion in the region. But where a vacuum has been created between society and the influence of the church in the matter of values, the disc jockeys and pop artists have moved in to claim the right to guide the minds of at least the youth. Unfortunately, this same popular culture has taken on the leadership role in vulgarizing colonial disengagement. Its lyrics make unabashed reference to sex and violence, and the dances it creates to match the lyrics are totally obscene, thriving on the exploitation of women. Some people charge that the general indiscipline among the young and the moral decadence among adults are due to the influence of certain realities in popular culture. Indeed if indigenizing theology once praised the significant role popular culture was playing in the kind of contextualization that represented Caribbean societies across cultural boundaries, it must now think twice. It seems that theology has a new duty to perform: to modify contextualization into less destructive demonstrations in society.

5. Some Conclusions

Because there are so many facets to the Caribbean reality, any conclusion regarding the religio-cultural situation will inevitably be complex, taking into consideration (1) faith as a principle and the varied forms its application takes; (2) self-understanding as a prerequisite for self-actualization; (3) the ramifications of disengagement — what is lost, what is gained and especially the consequences of extreme radicalism in the process; (4) post-colonial reconstruction and the way forward; (5) the way the gospel proves its relevance in the complexity of all this.

The faith that is in tension

The word "faith" is usually used in reference to belief in some kind of religious system; and theologians have spent an inordinate amount of time discussing its relation to reason. Karl Barth, for example, influenced by Anselm, discusses it in chronological order of theological method: first there is revelation, then faith apprehends revelation, and finally reason is employed to understand that which faith accepts. But Christianity is not the only place in which faith and understanding meet in this way. In Buddhism, for example, as one seeks spiritual growth and attains to it, faith has to be verified by experience. The fact is that there is a sense in which faith is relational among religions, in terms of meaning, intention and primary focus. If the relevance of the gospel in connection with Caribbean pluralism is to be addressed, it must be acknowledged that Christianity has no monopoly on faith.

Furthermore, if Justin Martyr, Leonardo Boff and many others are right in suggesting that "the gospel does not have its first beginnings only in the historical Jesus", we may be bold enough to conclude that faith which may be described as Christian can be found outside of the church. Consider the *logos*. One of the reasons — and perhaps the most plausible one — that Christianity made such an easy entry into the Graeco-Roman world was that that world was familiar with the *logos* principle long before Christian apologists used it. A clear example is the Jewish philosopher Philo the Alexandrian, who argued that since God is unknowable and indescribable, it is necessary to have a bridge between God and the world. The bridge that provided knowability is the divine *logos*. Philo, who was definitely not Christian, described the *logos* in such phrases such as "the first-born Son of God begotten of God", and "representative of humanity before God, our High Priest who supplicates for the corruptible before the incorruptible".

Philo, as a Jew, could not equate the *logos* with Christ, but when the early apologists did so, they meant that the *logos* as Jesus Christ was the basis of all that is. So when contemporary theologians pick the cosmological trend as a theme in Christology, they argue that Christ is at the basis of *all being*. Christ is then envisaged to have the same responsibility as the *logos* in the cosmos. What is more, cosmos comprises everything, Christian and un-Christian.

Even so, when faith is seen less in terms of abstract principle and more in relation to the universality of ethics, it becomes more functional, especially amidst the struggles of the developing world, of which the Caribbean is a part. In issues of ethics, faith calls into question injustice of one kind or another. Indeed, seeing faith in relation to ethical issues is not a new trend, because there is a universal understanding of religion according to which belief in and acceptance of transcendence usually work their way from the concreteness of ethics. Hence the faith tensions which have developed over religious forms in cross-cultural dynamics ought to serve the good purpose of being a source for indigenous and theological perspectives which give their blessings to Caribbean culture.

The importance of self-understanding

One of the marks of the achievement of self-actualization is the freedom to develop a value system. Autonomy is absolutely necessary if the development of values is to take place. According to Abraham Maslow, autonomy means being a self-governed agent of responsibility and self-discipline; when people are deprived of autonomy they can only be inferior instruments for the will and whim of the rest of society. In particular, the compensatory response that colonized and enslaved people must make sheerly for the sake of survival stifles developmental efforts and forces them to accept the values of others.

Self-understanding is a very important aspect of the reconstruction of the selfhood and self-will of people who have been under protracted periods of mind control. Part of this process of reconstruction is testing whether the values and the value system at work in the post-colonial situation are viable for the self-actualization and self-development of the people. In fact, as the Latin American liberation theologians used to point out, this is probably the most difficult part of reconstruction. When acculturation is long and severe, the host culture for reasons of survival internalizes the philosophy of the dominant culture to such an extent that it becomes almost innate. The standardization of moral precepts, the principles by which living is organized, concepts of beauty and interpretations of truth are internalized to the detriment of a *liberation philosophy* on the part of the host culture. And the most detrimental form this internalization takes is self-hatred. People hate themselves for not being what they have been socialized into considering normative.

The recovery of values is the recovery of selfhood, not only from the psychological but also from the theological perspective. From Bernard Lonergan we learn that value is a transcendental notion which addresses intentionality, and intentionality fosters self-transcendence. Self-transcendence, in this case, means that direct communication with the divine is heightened to the extent that human self-worth is fortified. This is what theologians mean when they talk about the appropriation of the *imago Dei*. This appropriation happens when marginalized people affirm the *being* that God has confirmed in them.

Of course in carrying out this whole process of self-understanding there is awareness of possible side-effects. Ultra-radicalism in the disengagement segment of self-understanding can cause the pendulum to swing to the other extreme. This is in no way to deny that there must be radicalism in disengagement; on the contrary, the very principle of disengagement is itself radical. If quietism were to control the principle of disengagement, nothing would be done and self-understanding would be postponed into "we shall know each other better by and by". The danger raised by ultra-radicalism is that of throwing out the baby with the bathwater. Values are so precious in self-development that if they are radicalized into meaninglessness, the efforts towards self-development will become just as meaningless. But there is enough evidence in the world of liberation movements to show that after radicalism rational adjustments can develop which make the potential values less vulnerable to self-destruction. And after passage of time, confrontation can be assumed through critical and transforming dialogue.

The gospel and interpretation

Parthians, Medes, Elamites, and residents of Mesopotamia, Judea and Cappadocia, Pontus and Asia, Phrygia and Pamphylia, Egypt and the parts of Libya belonging to Cyrene, and visitors from Rome, both Jews and proselytes, Cretians and Arabs — in our own languages we hear them speaking about God's deeds of power (Acts 2:9 11).

Peter, an apostle of Jesus Christ, to the resident exiles of the Dispersion in Pontus, Galatia, Cappadocia, Asia and Bithynia, who have been chosen and destined by God the Father and sanctified by the Spirit to be obedient to Jesus Christ and to be sprinkled with his blood... (1 Pet. 1:1 2).

Come to him, a living stone, though rejected by mortals yet chosen and precious in God's sight, and like living stones, let yourselves be built into a spiritual house, to be a holy priesthood, to offer spiritual sacrifices acceptable to God through Jesus Christ (1 Pet. 2:4 5).

What then is to be said about the gospel itself in its function in the Caribbean? Has it been shaped by any or all of the milieus of colonialism, disengagement and reconstruction, the search for self-understanding and unified cultural formation? Is the gospel expected to be apprehended by every single idiosyncrasy of that cultural milieu?

Some of these questions can be answered only over time, but one overarching response is that the gospel by its very nature is transcendent and transforming. As St Paul defined it, "it is the power of God for salvation to everyone who has faith" (Rom. 1:16). And in that definition, two important principles for the Caribbean reality stand out: *power* and *universality*.

1. *Power* as a principle is more easily experienced than defined, because definitions of it vary from discipline to discipline. It has been said that the simplest definition of power is "the ability to get things done". In theology "power" has a particular meaning, especially when it refers to divine omnipotence. However, in third-world liberation thought, divine power, while being taken as a given, has some bearing on the human condition. This understanding tends to draw on the ontological aspects of the meaning of power, referring to potency. Here Aristotle identified three distinguishing elements: power as source of change, capacity of performing and state of virtue. Power in this sense is related to praxis, since praxis connotes action determined to cause change in society. This is the definition which will influence thinking on how the gospel may impact anew the Caribbean reality.

Paul's mention of power in his definition of the gospel must be understood first of all in terms of its literal reference, because Paul is thinking not only that the gospel is self-authenticating, but also that its power is second to none other. The gospel is narrative, but it is also the proclamation of God's most powerful revelatory event, an act of love in which God appeared in human condition in a human situation for the sake of humanity.

Some argue that power is neutral and that what makes a serious difference is the *use* of it. This would seem to have been the understanding of the church in the New Testament, that power as a principle is donated by divine decree and that the exercise of it is good or bad depending on how it is used. Ironically, the New Testament church learned about the full effects of power as it was wielded by Rome, with its overwhelming power. In experiencing the power of Rome, the church came to understand that only the power of God through the gospel of Jesus Christ was able to override the imperial power. The first epistle of Peter typifies that under-standing. It was addressed to the resident aliens of Pontus, Galatia, Cappadocia, Asia and Bithynia — who by their migrant status resemble the Africans, Indians and Chinese in the Caribbean community. These people who, by virtue of their immigrant status, have no stake in Roman citizenship can be transformed by the power of the gospel into "a chosen race, a royal priesthood, a holy nation, God's own people" (1 Pet. 2:9). There is a tendency in the Caribbean to overlook the importance of the local elitist class which benefitted from colonialism and has succeeded in becoming the agent of neo-colonialism. This class has the power to manipulate the poor for their labour skills, thus creating a powerless mass, and it lives very well off that kind of exploitation. From the beginning this powerless mass, like Peter's resident aliens, have been allowed one purpose in life: to keep the economy moving — without being recognized for this. But in the case of the resident aliens in the Roman situation, the first epistle of Peter employs a brilliant analogy to demonstrate the positive effect of the power of the gospel. The point is that God has a place of permanence (a cornerstone), within the transience of "migrancy", for the recovery of strength and stability and dependability. This is not some spiritual illu-sion. This is a concrete and practical situation, because even in the strict classism of Rome, once in a while a statureless slave rose from the ashes of powerlessness into becoming a cornerstone of society.

So in a second sense, given the demonstration of divine power in the event, there is the natural conclusion that the best function of power is the empowerment of people. Liberation theologians have been saying this for some time. It is all well and good to say "Christ was made human that we might be made divine". If that statement does not come down to egalitarian considerations of the use of power in the world, it simply transfers the redress for powerlessness to other-worldly fulfilment.

2. *Universality* adds another dimension to the pervasiveness of the gospel. Hermeneutically speaking, the gospel narrative must be submitted to a three-dimensional principle of interpretation, assessing it for what it meant in its original situation of life, what it means for the present time and what it may mean "always". "Always" is the point at which the application transcends the locality of both time and space. So while the context is highly important for the identification and authentication of culture, the individual context exists within a larger reference. Otherwise God, whose concern the gospel represents, would be reduced to mere "tribal" significance.

The definition of the gospel as "the power of God for salvation to everyone who has faith" presents also a universal appeal which may be applied at two relating levels. Through the medium of faith everyone is included in the appeal of the gospel; yet "everyone" has to be seen in the same light as the Jamaican national motto to which we referred earlier: Out of Many One People.

The first level of universal appeal is contextual. The Caribbean cultural situation, despite its potential for unity, is not now in fact a melting-pot. There are the "many" as there is the "one". The point is that the appeal of the gospel addresses, one by one, with liberating care, each of the cultural forms that exist in the Caribbean.

While admitting that the gospel in Christian witness is *one*, it must also be acknowledged that its interpretation is pluriform. The very nature of the world in which the gospel exists demands that concession. The world is multi-cultured. Each culture, in the validity of its psychological, spiritual and social development, forms its individual insights as a tool for interpretation. The gospel, therefore, has no choice but to face the risk of interpretation, as subjective as that prospect may be. The Pentecost experience in Acts 2 would be a waste of time if this were not true. For since language is at the very heart of culture, people hear more in the multifarious expressions of the gospel than mere differences in linguistic vocabulary. They hear the gospel address their own cultural particularity. This means that the need for the gospel to risk interpretation in terms of cultural peculiarities is only one side of the story. The other side is that the gospel truly has the capacity to address the peculiarity of culture, whatever that culture may be.

So as the Caribbean comprises multiple cultural roots and multiple religious forms, the gospel addresses them all and offers them the potential for contextual unity.

Even without uniformity there is then the second universal level at which the gospel operates. This is what Walbert Buhlmann refers to as "creation covenant": the point at which the gospel takes individual contexts into a global arena. Individual contexts derive authenticity out of divine creativity, and creation is a universal concept.

Self-understanding is of paramount importance to those who must seek and find it. But the ultimate aim of contextual distinction is to determine what each particular context may contribute to the whole household of God.

Selected Bibliography

Dale Bisnauth, *History of Religions in the Caribbean*, Kingston, Kingston Publishers, 1989.

Oscar L. Bolioli, ed., *The Caribbean: Culture of Resistance, Spirit of Hope*, New York, Friendship Press, 1993.

Walbert Buhlmann, *God's Chosen Peoples*, Maryknoll NY, Orbis, 1982.

Brian Gates, ed., *Afro-Caribbean Religions*, London, Ward Lock Educational, 1980.

Richard Gray, *Black Christians and White Missionaries*, New Haven, Yale U.P., 1990.

Melville J. Herskovits, *The Myth of the Negro Past*, Boston, Beacon Press, 1958.

Bernard Lonergan, *Method in Theology*, New York, Herder & Herder, 1973.

Abraham H. Maslow, *Motivation and Personality*, New York, Harper & Row, 1970.

M. Douglas Meeks, *God the Economist*, Minneapolis, Fortress Press, 1989.

Ivor Morrish, *Obeah, Christ and Rastaman*, London, James Clarke, 1982.

Luis N. Rivera, *A Violent Evangelism: The Political and Religious Conquest of the Americas*, Louisville, John Knox Press, 1990.

Lewin L. Williams, *Caribbean Theology*, New York, Peter Lang, 1994.